Collecting Seashells

by Ainslie Mitchell
illustrated by Anna Walker

Harcourt
SCHOOL PUBLISHERS

Printed in Mexico

ISBN 10: 0-15-349999-0
ISBN 13: 978-0-15-349999-9

Ordering Options
ISBN 10: 0-15-349937-0 (Grade 2 ELL Collection)
ISBN 13: 978-0-15-349937-1 (Grade 2 ELL Collection)
ISBN 10: 0-15-357238-8 (package of 5)
ISBN 13: 978-0-15-357238-8 (package of 5)

1 2 3 4 5 6 7 8 9 10   050   15 14 13 12 11 10 09 08 07 06

Gran lived by the beach. Katie often
went to stay with her during vacation.
Katie really liked visiting Gran.

Katie liked walking on the sand and splashing in the waves. She liked talking with Gran more than anything. Gran was never too busy to listen.

Katie and Gran were at the beach one
day. They were making a sand castle.

"My friend Maisie collects toy dogs,"
said Katie. "My friend John collects stamps.
I don't collect anything."

5

Gran was putting shells on the sand castle. She held up a shell. "You could collect empty houses," she said.

"What do you mean?" asked Katie.

"I mean seashells," laughed Gran. "Sea animals once lived in these shells."

"That's a great idea!" said Katie. "I'm going to collect seashells."

Katie picked up a pretty shell from the pile she and Gran had collected. That was how Katie started collecting shells.

Gran and Katie went shopping the
next day. Gran bought some small boxes
for Katie. Katie put a different kind of
shell in each box.

Katie put shells that looked like snail shells in a red box. She put the biggest snail shell to her ear. She thought she could hear the sea!

Katie put flat shells in a blue box.
Some were round, and some looked like
little fans.

Katie collected shells of many different colors. She learned the names of the shells. She learned what animal had once lived in each shell.

Katie put each box of shells on a shelf. She made a sign that said, "My Empty House Collection."

Katie's friend Maisie came to visit.
"How can you fit empty houses in boxes?"
asked Maisie.

   "They are not real houses," laughed
Katie. "They are animal houses. They are
seashells!"

"Wow!" said Maisie. "Can we go and find some seashells together?"

"That would be fun," said Katie.

"Come on," said Gran. "Let's collect some seashells. Perhaps Maisie can start a collection, too."

Scaffolded Language Development

DESCRIBING WORDS Review describing words with children. Remind them that describing words can tell about nouns (people, places, animals, things). Discuss with children words in the book that tell about the shells, such as *snail, pretty, flat.* Then hold up some classroom objects, such as a pencil, some colored paper, and a book. Invite children to say appropriate words to describe these objects. Using the words children suggest, write sentences on the board. For example, *This is a red pencil. The paper is green. The book is new.* Have children chorally say the sentences. Then invite children to replace the describing words with other appropriate describing words.

Science

Make a Chart Remind children that Katie sorted her shells into different types. Have children write the heads *Sea Animals with Shells* and *Sea Animals without Shells.* Guide children in writing appropriate animals under each head.

 School-Home Connection

Talk About Collecting Have children talk to family members about the book. Then talk about the things they like to collect. Encourage children to ask family members how the interest developed.

Word Count: 324